# Dump Cakes
## & One-Bowl Baking

Publications International, Ltd.

*Favorite Brand Name Recipes* is a trademark of Publications International, Ltd.

**Pictured on the front cover:** Peach Strawberry Cake *(page 20).*

**Pictured on the back cover** *(clockwise from top):* Carrot Banana Cake
*(page 78),* Double Banana Cake *(page 56)* and Blackberry Almond Cake
*(page 46).*

ISBN: 978-1-68022-031-5

Library of Congress Control Number: 2013949289

Manufactured in China.

8 7 6 5 4 3 2 1

**Microwave Cooking:** Microwave ovens vary in wattage. Use the cooking
times as guidelines and check for doneness before adding more time.

Publications International, Ltd.

# CONTENTS

# CLASSIC
## DUMP CAKES

### PEACH MELBA DUMP CAKE

- 2 cans (21 ounces each) peach pie filling
- 1 package (12 ounces) frozen raspberries, thawed and drained
- 1 package (about 15 ounces) yellow cake mix
- ½ cup (1 stick) butter, cut into thin slices
- Ice cream (optional)

**1.** Preheat oven to 350°F. Spray 13×9-inch baking pan with nonstick cooking spray.

**2.** Spread peach pie filling in prepared pan; sprinkle with raspberries. Top with cake mix, spreading evenly. Top with butter in single layer, covering cake mix as much as possible.

**3.** Bake 40 to 45 minutes or until toothpick inserted into center of cake comes out clean. Cool at least 15 minutes before serving. Serve with ice cream, if desired.

*Makes 12 to 16 servings*

# DOUBLE PINEAPPLE BERRY CAKE

  1  can (20 ounces) crushed pineapple, undrained

  1  package (12 ounces) frozen mixed berries,
      thawed and drained

  1  package (about 18 ounces) pineapple cake mix

  ½  cup (1 stick) butter, cut into thin slices

     Whipped cream (optional)

**1.** Preheat oven to 350°F. Spray 13×9-inch baking pan with nonstick cooking spray.

**2.** Spread pineapple and berries in prepared pan. Top with cake mix, spreading evenly. Top with butter in single layer, covering cake mix as much as possible.

**3.** Bake 45 to 50 minutes or until toothpick inserted into center of cake comes out clean. Cool at least 15 minutes before serving. Serve with whipped cream, if desired.

*Makes 12 to 16 servings*

# SIMPLE S'MORE CAKE

   1 package (about 15 ounces) milk chocolate cake mix
   1 package (4-serving size) chocolate instant pudding
       and pie filling mix
1½ cups milk
   1 package (10 ounces) mini marshmallows
   1 cup milk chocolate chips *or* 2 (4-ounce) milk chocolate
       bars, broken into pieces
   5 whole graham crackers, broken into bite-size pieces

1. Preheat oven to 350°F. Spray 13×9-inch baking pan with nonstick cooking spray.

2. Combine cake mix, pudding mix and milk in large bowl; beat 1 to 2 minutes or until well blended. Spread batter in prepared pan.

3. Bake 30 to 35 minutes or until toothpick inserted into center comes out clean. *Turn oven to broil.*

4. Sprinkle marshmallows, chocolate chips and graham crackers over cake. Broil 6 inches from heat source 30 seconds to 1 minute or until marshmallows are golden brown. Cool at least 15 minutes before serving.

*Makes 12 to 16 servings*

# Banana Split Cake

1 can (20 ounces) crushed pineapple, undrained

1 can (14½ ounces) tart cherries in water, drained

1 package (about 18 ounces) banana cake mix

½ cup (1 stick) butter, cut into thin slices

½ cup semisweet chocolate chips

½ cup chopped pecans

Whipped cream and maraschino cherries (optional)

**1.** Preheat oven to 350°F. Spray 13×9-inch baking pan with nonstick cooking spray.

**2.** Spread pineapple and tart cherries in prepared pan. Top with cake mix, spreading evenly. Top with butter in single layer, covering cake mix as much as possible. Sprinkle with chocolate chips and pecans.

**3.** Bake 55 to 60 minutes or until toothpick inserted into center of cake comes out clean. Cool at least 15 minutes before serving. Top with whipped cream and maraschino cherries, if desired.

*Makes 12 to 16 servings*

# Apple Peach Dump Cake

- 2 cans (21 ounces each) apple pie filling
- 2 cans (15 ounces each) peach slices, drained
- 1 teaspoon ground cinnamon, divided
- ½ teaspoon ground nutmeg, divided
- 1 package (about 15 ounces) white cake mix
- ½ cup (1 stick) butter, melted

1. Preheat oven to 350°F. Spray 13×9-inch baking pan with nonstick cooking spray.

2. Spread apple pie filling and peaches in prepared pan. Sprinkle with ½ teaspoon cinnamon and ¼ teaspoon nutmeg. Top with cake mix, spreading evenly. Pour butter over top, covering cake mix as much as possible. Sprinkle with remaining ½ teaspoon cinnamon and ¼ teaspoon nutmeg.

3. Bake 1 hour or until top is lightly browned and toothpick inserted into center of cake comes out clean. Cool at least 15 minutes before serving.

*Makes 12 to 16 servings*

# PINEAPPLE ANGEL CAKE

> 2 cups fresh or thawed frozen sliced strawberries
>
> 1 can (20 ounces) crushed pineapple, undrained
>
> 1 package (16 ounces) angel food cake mix

**1.** Preheat oven to 350°F.

**2.** Spread strawberries in 13×9-inch baking pan. Combine pineapple and cake mix in large bowl; beat 1 to 2 minutes or until well blended. Spread batter evenly over strawberries.

**3.** Bake 35 to 40 minutes or until toothpick inserted into center comes out clean. Cool in pan at least 30 minutes before serving.

*Makes 12 to 16 servings*

# Super Fruity Confetti Cake

2  cans (15 ounces each) fruit cocktail, drained

1  package (about 15 ounces) white cake mix

½  cup (1 stick) butter, cut into thin slices

¼  cup multicolored tiny crunchy tangy candies

**1.** Preheat oven to 350°F. Spray 13×9-inch baking pan with nonstick cooking spray.

**2.** Spread fruit cocktail in prepared pan. Top with cake mix, spreading evenly. Top with butter in single layer, covering cake mix as much as possible.

**3.** Bake 45 to 50 minutes or until toothpick inserted into center of cake comes out clean, sprinkling with candies during last 20 minutes of baking. Cool at least 15 minutes before serving.

*Makes 12 to 16 servings*

# ORANGE PINEAPPLE COCONUT CAKE

- 1 can (20 ounces) crushed pineapple, undrained
- 1 can (15 ounces) mandarin oranges in light syrup, drained
- 1½ cups flaked coconut, divided
- 1 package (about 15 ounces) vanilla cake mix
- ½ cup (1 stick) butter, cut into thin slices

1. Preheat oven to 350°F. Spray 13×9-inch baking pan with nonstick cooking spray.

2. Spread pineapple and mandarin oranges in prepared pan; sprinkle with ½ cup coconut. Top with cake mix, spreading evenly. Top with butter in single layer, covering cake mix as much as possible. Sprinkle with remaining 1 cup coconut.

3. Bake 45 to 50 minutes or until toothpick inserted into center of cake comes out clean. Cool at least 15 minutes before serving.

*Makes 12 to 16 servings*

# PINK LEMONADE CAKE

3 cups fresh or thawed frozen sliced strawberries

¼ cup powdered pink lemonade mix

1 package (about 15 ounces) white cake mix

½ cup (1 stick) butter, cut into thin slices

½ cup water

1. Preheat oven to 350°F. Spray 9-inch square baking pan with nonstick cooking spray.

2. Spread strawberries in prepared pan; sprinkle with lemonade mix. Top with cake mix, spreading evenly. Top with butter in single layer. Slowly pour water over top, covering cake mix as much as possible.

3. Bake 40 to 45 minutes or until toothpick inserted into center of cake comes out clean. Cool at least 15 minutes before serving.

*Makes 9 servings*

# PEACH STRAWBERRY CAKE

1 can (29 ounces) peach slices in light syrup, undrained

1½ cups frozen sliced strawberries, thawed and drained

1 package (about 15 ounces) yellow cake mix

½ cup (1 stick) butter, melted

Ice cream (optional)

**1.** Preheat oven to 350°F. Spray 13×9-inch baking pan with nonstick cooking spray.

**2.** Spread peaches and strawberries in prepared pan. Top with cake mix, spreading evenly. Pour butter over top, covering cake mix as much as possible.

**3.** Bake 50 to 55 minutes or until toothpick inserted into center of cake comes out clean. Cool at least 15 minutes before serving. Serve with ice cream, if desired.

*Makes 12 to 16 servings*

# MIXED BERRY DUMP CAKE

- 2 packages (12 ounces each) frozen mixed berries, thawed and drained
- 1 package (about 15 ounces) white cake mix
- ¼ teaspoon ground cinnamon
- 1 can (12 ounces) lemon-lime soda
- ½ cup cinnamon chips

1. Preheat oven to 350°F. Spray 13×9-inch baking pan with nonstick cooking spray.

2. Spread mixed berries in prepared pan. Top with cake mix, spreading evenly. Sprinkle with cinnamon. Slowly pour soda over top, covering cake mix as much as possible. Sprinkle with cinnamon chips.

3. Bake 45 to 50 minutes or until toothpick inserted into center of cake comes out clean. Cool at least 15 minutes before serving.

*Makes 12 to 16 servings*

# CHA-CHA-CHA CHERRY CAKE

2 packages (12 ounces each) frozen cherries, thawed and drained

1 package (4-serving size) cherry gelatin

1 package (about 15 ounces) white cake mix

½ cup (1 stick) butter, cut into thin slices

1 cup chopped walnuts

¼ cup water

1. Preheat oven to 350°F. Spray 9-inch square baking pan with nonstick cooking spray.

2. Spread cherries in prepared pan; sprinkle with gelatin. Top with cake mix, spreading evenly. Top with butter in single layer, covering cake mix as much as possible. Sprinkle with walnuts. Drizzle water over top.

3. Bake 50 to 60 minutes or until toothpick inserted into center of cake comes out clean. Cool at least 15 minutes before serving.

*Makes 9 servings*

# Tropical Dump Cake

- 1 can (20 ounces) crushed pineapple, undrained
- 1 can (15 ounces) peach slices in light syrup, undrained
- 1 package (about 15 ounces) yellow cake mix
- ½ cup (1 stick) butter, cut into thin slices
- 1 cup packed brown sugar
- ½ cup flaked coconut
- ½ cup chopped pecans

1. Preheat oven to 350°F. Spray 13×9-inch pan with nonstick cooking spray.

2. Spread pineapple and peaches in prepared pan. Top with cake mix, spreading evenly. Top with butter in single layer, covering cake mix as much as possible. Sprinkle with brown sugar, coconut and pecans.

3. Bake 40 to 45 minutes or until toothpick inserted into center of cake comes out clean. Cool at least 15 minutes before serving.

*Makes 12 to 16 servings*

# BLUEBERRY CINNAMON CAKE

2 packages (12 ounces each) frozen blueberries, thawed and drained

⅓ cup sugar

¾ teaspoon ground cinnamon, divided

1 package (about 15 ounces) yellow cake mix

¾ cup (1½ sticks) butter, cut into thin slices

Ice cream (optional)

**1.** Preheat oven to 350°F. Spray 13×9-inch baking pan with nonstick cooking spray.

**2.** Spread blueberries in prepared pan. Sprinkle with sugar and ½ teaspoon cinnamon; toss to coat. Top with cake mix, spreading evenly. Top with butter in single layer, covering cake mix as much as possible. Sprinkle with remaining ¼ teaspoon cinnamon.

**3.** Bake 50 to 60 minutes or until toothpick inserted into center of cake comes out clean. Cool at least 15 minutes before serving. Serve with ice cream, if desired.

*Makes 12 to 16 servings*

# Super Strawberry Cake

3 cups thawed frozen or fresh strawberries,
cut into halves or quarters

1 package (about 15 ounces) strawberry cake mix

½ cup (1 stick) butter, cut into thin slices

Whipped cream (optional)

**1.** Preheat oven to 350°F. Spray 13×9-inch baking pan with nonstick cooking spray.

**2.** Spread strawberries in prepared pan. Top with cake mix, spreading evenly. Top with butter in single layer, covering cake mix as much as possible.

**3.** Bake 45 to 50 minutes or until toothpick inserted into center of cake comes out clean. Cool at least 15 minutes before serving. Serve with whipped cream, if desired.

*Makes 12 to 16 servings*

# FAMILY
## FAVORITES

### CHERRY CHEESECAKE DUMP CAKE

- 1 can (21 ounces) cherry pie filling
- 1 can (14½ ounces) tart cherries in water, drained
- 4 ounces cream cheese, cut into small pieces
- 1 package (about 15 ounces) yellow cake mix
- ½ cup (1 stick) butter, cut into thin slices

1. Preheat oven to 350°F. Spray 13×9-inch baking pan with nonstick cooking spray.

2. Spread cherry pie filling and tart cherries in prepared pan. Scatter cream cheese pieces over cherries. Top with cake mix, spreading evenly. Top with butter in single layer, covering cake mix as much as possible.

3. Bake 45 to 50 minutes or until toothpick inserted into center of cake comes out clean. Cool at least 15 minutes before serving.

*Makes 12 to 16 servings*

# TEMPTING TURTLE CAKE

 1 package (about 15 ounces) devil's food cake mix

 1 package (4-serving size) chocolate instant pudding and pie filling mix

 1½ cups milk

 1 cup chopped caramels

 1 cup semisweet chocolate chips

 ½ cup pecan pieces

 ½ teaspoon coarse salt (optional)

1. Preheat oven to 350°F. Spray 13×9-inch baking pan with nonstick cooking spray.

2. Combine cake mix, pudding mix and milk in large bowl; beat 1 to 2 minutes or until well blended. Spread batter in prepared pan; top with caramels, chocolate chips and pecans. Sprinkle with salt, if desired.

3. Bake 30 to 35 minutes or until toothpick inserted into center comes out clean. Cool at least 15 minutes before serving.

*Makes 12 to 16 servings*

# APRICOT DOUBLE CHIP CAKE

- 2 cups apricot preserves or jam
- ½ cup semisweet chocolate chips, divided
- ½ cup white chocolate chips, divided
- 1 package (about 15 ounces) yellow cake mix
- ½ cup (1 stick) butter, cut into thin slices
- ⅓ cup water

1. Preheat oven to 350°F. Spray 9-inch square baking pan with nonstick cooking spray.

2. Spread preserves in prepared pan. Sprinkle with half of semisweet chips and half of white chips. Top with cake mix, spreading evenly. Top with butter in single layer, covering cake mix as much as possible. Drizzle water over top. Sprinkle with remaining semisweet and white chips.

3. Bake 50 to 55 minutes or until toothpick inserted into center of cake comes out clean. Cool at least 15 minutes before serving.

*Makes 9 servings*

# Red Velvet White Chip Cake

  1  package (about 18 ounces) red velvet cake mix
  1  package (4-serving size) vanilla instant pudding
       and pie filling mix
1½  cups milk
  2  ounces cream cheese, cut into small pieces
  ½  cup white chocolate chips

**1.** Preheat oven to 350°F. Spray 13×9-inch baking pan with nonstick cooking spray.

**2.** Combine cake mix, pudding mix and milk in medium bowl; beat 1 to 2 minutes or until well blended. Spread batter in prepared pan; sprinkle with cream cheese and white chips.

**3.** Bake 25 to 30 minutes or until toothpick inserted into center comes out clean. Cool in pan on wire rack. Serve warm or at room temperature.

*Makes 12 to 16 servings*

# RASPBERRY LOVERS' DUMP CAKE

  1  can (21 ounces) raspberry pie filling

  1  package (12 ounces) frozen raspberries, thawed and drained

  1  package (12 ounces) semisweet chocolate chips, divided

  1  package (about 15 ounces) white cake mix

  ¾  cup (1½ sticks) butter, cut into thin slices

  ½  cup packed brown sugar

     Ice cream (optional)

**1.** Preheat oven to 350°F. Spray 13×9-inch baking pan with nonstick cooking spray.

**2.** Spread raspberry pie filling in prepared pan; sprinkle with raspberries. Sprinkle with half of chocolate chips. Top with cake mix, spreading evenly. Top with butter in single layer, covering cake mix as much as possible. Sprinkle with brown sugar and remaining chocolate chips.

**3.** Bake 50 to 60 minutes or until golden brown and toothpick inserted into center of cake comes out clean. Cool at least 15 minutes before serving. Serve with ice cream, if desired.

*Makes 12 to 16 servings*

# CARAMEL CANDY CAKE

  1  package (about 15 ounces) yellow cake mix

  2  eggs

  ½  cup (1 stick) butter, melted

  ½  cup milk

  1  package (8 ounces) unwrapped bite-size chocolate peanut caramel candies, chopped, divided

  2  tablespoons caramel topping, warmed

**1.** Preheat oven to 350°F. Spray 9-inch square baking pan with nonstick cooking spray.

**2.** Combine cake mix, eggs, butter and milk in large bowl; beat 1 to 2 minutes or until well blended. Stir in half of candy. Spread batter in prepared pan; sprinkle with remaining candy. Drizzle with caramel topping.

**3.** Bake 30 to 35 minutes or until toothpick inserted into center comes out clean. Cool in pan at least 15 minutes before serving.

*Makes 9 servings*

# Black Forest Cake

2 cans (21 ounces each) cherry pie filling

1 package (about 15 ounces) chocolate fudge cake mix

¾ cup semisweet chocolate chips

¾ cup (1½ sticks) butter, melted

1. Preheat oven to 350°F. Spray 13×9-inch baking pan with nonstick cooking spray.

2. Spread cherry pie filling in prepared pan. Top with cake mix, spreading evenly. Sprinkle with chocolate chips. Pour butter over top, covering cake mix as much as possible.

3. Bake 30 to 35 minutes or until toothpick inserted into center of cake comes out clean. Cool at least 15 minutes before serving.

*Makes 12 to 16 servings*

# BANANA STRAWBERRY DUMP CAKE

1 can (21 ounces) strawberry pie filling

1 can (20 ounces) crushed pineapple, undrained

1 package (about 18 ounces) banana cake mix

½ cup (1 stick) butter, cut into thin slices

1. Preheat oven to 350°F. Spray 13×9-inch baking pan with nonstick cooking spray.

2. Spread strawberry pie filling and pineapple in prepared pan. Top with cake mix, spreading evenly. Top with butter in single layer, covering cake mix as much as possible.

3. Bake 45 to 50 minutes or until toothpick inserted into center of cake comes out clean. Cool at least 15 minutes before serving.

*Makes 12 to 16 servings*

# BLACKBERRY ALMOND CAKE

- 2 packages (12 ounces each) frozen blackberries, thawed and drained
- ¼ cup granulated sugar
- 1 package (about 15 ounces) yellow cake mix
- ¾ cup (1½ sticks) butter, cut into thin slices
- ½ cup sliced almonds
- ¼ cup packed brown sugar

1. Preheat oven to 350°F. Spray 13×9-inch baking pan with nonstick cooking spray.

2. Spread blackberries in prepared pan; sprinkle with granulated sugar and toss to coat. Top with cake mix, spreading evenly. Top with butter in single layer, covering cake mix as much as possible. Sprinkle with almonds and brown sugar.

3. Bake 50 to 60 minutes or until toothpick inserted into center of cake comes out clean. Cool at least 15 minutes before serving.

*Makes 12 to 16 servings*

# LEMON BLUEBERRY CAKE

- 1 package (about 18 ounces) lemon cake mix
- 1 package (4-serving size) lemon instant pudding and pie filling mix
- 4 eggs
- ¾ cup water
- ½ cup vegetable or canola oil
- 1 cup fresh blueberries, divided

**1.** Preheat oven to 350°F. Spray 13×9-inch baking pan with nonstick cooking spray.

**2.** Combine cake mix, pudding mix, eggs, water and oil in large bowl; beat 1 to 2 minutes or until well blended. Gently fold in ½ cup blueberries. Spread batter in prepared pan; sprinkle with remaining ½ cup blueberries.

**3.** Bake 20 to 25 minutes or until toothpick inserted into center comes out clean. Cool completely in pan on wire rack.

*Makes 12 to 16 servings*

# Island Delight Cake

3 ripe mangoes, peeled and cubed (about 4½ cups)

1 package (about 18 ounces) pineapple cake mix

1 can (12 ounces) lemon-lime or orange soda

½ cup chopped macadamia nuts (optional)

1. Preheat oven to 350°F. Spray 13×9-inch baking pan with nonstick cooking spray.

2. Spread mangoes in prepared pan. Top with cake mix, spreading evenly. Pour soda over top, covering cake mix as much as possible. Sprinkle with macadamia nuts, if desired.

3. Bake 35 to 40 minutes or until toothpick inserted into center of cake comes out clean. Cool at least 15 minutes before serving.

*Makes 12 to 16 servings*

# Rainbow Dump Cake

    1  can (20 ounces) crushed pineapple, undrained
    1  can (14½ ounces) tart cherries in water, drained
    1  package (about 15 ounces) yellow cake mix
    ½  cup (1 stick) butter, cut into thin slices
    ½  cup candy-coated chocolate pieces

**1.** Preheat oven to 350°F. Spray 13×9-inch baking pan with nonstick cooking spray.

**2.** Spread pineapple and cherries in prepared pan. Top with cake mix, spreading evenly. Top with butter in single layer, covering cake mix as much as possible.

**3.** Bake 35 to 40 minutes or until toothpick inserted into center of cake comes out clean, sprinkling with chocolate pieces during last 10 minutes of baking. Cool at least 15 minutes before serving.

*Makes 12 to 16 servings*

# Peach Cranberry Upside Down Cake

- ¼ cup (½ stick) butter, melted
- ½ cup packed brown sugar
- 3 cups thawed frozen or canned peach slices (thick slices cut in half)
- 2 cups fresh or thawed frozen cranberries
- 1 package (about 15 ounces) yellow cake mix, plus ingredients to prepare mix

1. Preheat oven to 350°F. Spray two 9-inch round cake pans with nonstick cooking spray.

2. Divide butter and brown sugar between prepared pans; spread evenly over bottom of pans. Arrange peach slices over butter mixture; sprinkle with cranberries.

3. Prepare cake mix according to package directions. Spread batter over fruit in each pan.

4. Bake 30 to 35 minutes or until toothpick inserted into center of cakes comes out clean. Cool 5 minutes; invert cakes onto serving plates. Cool at least 30 minutes before serving.

*Makes 12 to 16 servings*

# Double Banana Cake

1　package (about 18 ounces) banana cake mix, plus
　　ingredients to prepare mix

¾　cup chopped hazelnuts or sliced almonds, toasted,*
　　divided

1　banana, thinly sliced

¼　cup chocolate hazelnut spread, warmed**

*To toast hazelnuts, spread in single layer on baking sheet. Bake in
preheated 350°F oven 5 to 7 minutes or until golden brown, stirring
frequently.

**Microwave on LOW (30%) about 1 minute or until pourable.

1. Preheat oven to 350°F. Spray 9-inch square baking pan
with nonstick cooking spray.

2. Prepare cake mix according to package directions; stir
in ½ cup hazelnuts. Spread half of batter in prepared pan.
Top with banana slices; drizzle with 2 tablespoons chocolate
hazelnut spread. Top with remaining half of batter; sprinkle
with remaining ¼ cup hazelnuts and drizzle with 2 tablespoons
chocolate hazelnut spread.

3. Bake 25 to 30 minutes or until toothpick inserted into
center comes out clean. Cool in pan at least 15 minutes
before serving.

*Makes 9 servings*

# FALL
## FLAVORS

## CRANBERRY APPLE CAKE

1 can (21 ounces) apple pie filling

1 can (14 ounces) whole berry cranberry sauce

1 package (about 15 ounces) yellow cake mix

½ cup (1 stick) butter, cut into thin slices

½ cup chopped walnuts

**1.** Preheat oven to 350°F. Spray 13×9-inch baking pan with nonstick cooking spray.

**2.** Spread apple pie filling in prepared pan; top with cranberry sauce. Top with cake mix, spreading evenly. Top with butter in single layer, covering cake mix as much as possible. Sprinkle with walnuts.

**3.** Bake 50 to 55 minutes or until toothpick inserted into center of cake comes out clean. Cool at least 15 minutes before serving.

*Makes 12 to 16 servings*

# PUMPKIN PECAN CAKE

     1  **can (15 ounces) solid-pack pumpkin**

     1  **can (12 ounces) evaporated milk**

     1  **cup packed brown sugar**

     3  **eggs**

     2  **teaspoons pumpkin pie spice**

     ½  **teaspoon salt**

     1  **package (about 15 ounces) yellow cake mix**

     ¾  **cup (1½ sticks) butter, cut into thin slices**

     ½  **cup pecan halves**

1. Preheat oven to 350°F. Spray 13×9-inch baking pan with nonstick cooking spray.

2. Combine pumpkin, evaporated milk, brown sugar, eggs, pumpkin pie spice and salt in large bowl; beat until well blended. Pour into prepared pan. Top with cake mix, spreading evenly. Top with butter in single layer, covering cake mix as much as possible. Sprinkle with pecans.

3. Bake about 1 hour or until toothpick inserted into center of cake comes out clean. Cool completely in pan on wire rack.

*Makes 18 servings*

# Granola Caramel Carrot Cake

1  can (20 ounces) crushed pineapple, undrained

1  package (about 15 ounces) carrot cake mix

½  cup (1 stick) butter, cut into thin slices

1  cup granola

3  tablespoons caramel topping, warmed

   Ice cream (optional)

1. Preheat oven to 350°F. Spray 13×9-inch baking pan with nonstick cooking spray.

2. Spread pineapple in prepared pan. Top with cake mix, spreading evenly. Top with butter in single layer, covering cake mix as much as possible. Sprinkle with granola; drizzle with caramel topping.

3. Bake 50 to 55 minutes or until toothpick inserted into center of cake comes out clean. Cool at least 15 minutes before serving. Serve with ice cream, if desired.

*Makes 12 to 16 servings*

# Sweet Potato Cake

    1  can (29 ounces) sweet potatoes, drained
    1  package (about 15 ounces) yellow cake mix
    3  eggs
  1½  teaspoons apple pie spice, plus additional
       for top of cake
    ⅔  cup chopped nuts, divided

1. Preheat oven to 350°F. Spray 13×9-inch baking pan with nonstick cooking spray.

2. Place sweet potatoes in large bowl; mash with fork. Add cake mix, eggs and apple pie spice; beat 1 to 2 minutes or until well blended. Stir in ⅓ cup nuts. Spread batter in prepared pan; sprinkle with remaining ⅓ cup nuts and additional apple pie spice.

3. Bake 30 to 35 minutes or until toothpick inserted into center comes out clean. Cool in pan at least 15 minutes before serving.

*Makes 12 to 16 servings*

# Orange Cranberry Cake

  1  package (about 15 ounces) yellow cake mix

  4  eggs

  ¾  cup orange juice

  ½  cup vegetable or canola oil

  ¼  cup water

  1  cup dried cranberries

     Powdered sugar (optional)

1. Preheat oven to 350°F. Grease and flour 12-cup (10-inch) bundt pan.

2. Combine cake mix, eggs, orange juice, oil and water in large bowl; beat 1 to 2 minutes or until well blended. Stir in cranberries. Pour batter into prepared pan.

3. Bake about 40 minutes or until toothpick inserted near center comes out clean. Cool in pan 10 minutes; invert onto wire rack to cool completely.

4. Sprinkle with powdered sugar just before serving, if desired.

*Makes 12 servings*

# Sweet-Hot Apple Dump Cake

 2  cans (21 ounces each) apple pie filling

 ¼  cup plus 2 tablespoons hot cinnamon candies, divided

 1  package (about 15 ounces) yellow cake mix

 ½  cup (1 stick) butter, cut into thin slices

**1.** Preheat oven to 350°F. Spray 13×9-inch baking pan with nonstick cooking spray.

**2.** Spread apple pie filling in prepared pan. Sprinkle with ¼ cup cinnamon candies. Top with cake mix, spreading evenly. Top with butter in single layer, covering cake mix as much as possible.

**3.** Bake 45 to 55 minutes or until toothpick inserted into center of cake comes out clean, sprinkling with remaining 2 tablespoons cinnamon candies during last 10 minutes of baking. Cool at least 15 minutes before serving.

*Makes 12 to 16 servings*

# TRIPLE GINGER PEAR CAKE

 2  cans (29 ounces each) pear slices in light syrup, undrained

 ⅓  cup finely chopped crystallized ginger

 ¼  teaspoon ground ginger

 1  package (about 15 ounces) yellow cake mix

 ½  cup (1 stick) butter, cut into thin slices

 1  cup crumbled gingersnaps (about 16 cookies)

1. Preheat oven to 350°F. Spray 13×9-inch baking pan with nonstick cooking spray.

2. Drain pears, reserving 1 cup syrup. Cut pear slices into ¾-inch chunks with paring knife or scissors. Combine pears and reserved syrup in prepared pan; sprinkle with crystallized ginger and ground ginger. Top with cake mix, spreading evenly. Top with butter in single layer, covering cake mix as much as possible. Sprinkle with gingersnap crumbs.

3. Bake 40 to 45 minutes or until toothpick inserted into center of cake comes out clean. Cool at least 15 minutes before serving.

*Makes 12 to 16 servings*

# CRANBERRY COBBLER CAKE

- 1 can (14 ounces) whole berry cranberry sauce
- 1 package (9 ounces) yellow cake mix
- ¼ cup (½ stick) butter, melted
- ½ cup granola

**1.** Preheat oven to 350°F. Spray 9-inch pie plate with nonstick cooking spray.

**2.** Spread cranberries in prepared pie plate. Top with cake mix, spreading evenly. Pour butter over top, covering cake mix as much as possible. Sprinkle with granola.

**3.** Bake 55 to 60 minutes or until toothpick inserted into center of cake comes out clean. Cool at least 15 minutes before serving.

*Makes 6 to 8 servings*

# APPLE PIE DUMP CAKE

   1  can (21 ounces) apple pie filling

   1  package (about 15 ounces) white cake mix

   3  eggs

   ½  cup vegetable or canola oil

   ⅓  cup chopped pecans

1. Preheat oven to 350°F. Spray 13×9-inch baking pan with nonstick cooking spray.

2. Place apple pie filling in large bowl; cut apple slices into chunks with paring knife or scissors. Add cake mix, eggs and oil; beat 1 to 2 minutes or until well blended. Spread batter in prepared pan; sprinkle with pecans.

3. Bake 40 to 45 minutes or until toothpick inserted into center comes out clean. Cool in pan at least 15 minutes before serving.

*Makes 12 to 16 servings*

# Caramel Apple Peanut Cake

  2  cans (21 ounces each) apple pie filling

 ½  cup lightly salted peanuts, divided

  1  package (about 15 ounces) yellow cake mix

 ½  cup (1 stick) butter, cut into thin slices

 ⅓  cup caramel topping, warmed

**1.** Preheat oven to 350°F. Spray 13×9-inch baking pan with nonstick cooking spray.

**2.** Spread apple pie filling in prepared pan; sprinkle with ¼ cup peanuts. Top with cake mix, spreading evenly. Top with butter in single layer, covering cake mix as much as possible. Drizzle with caramel topping; sprinkle with remaining ¼ cup peanuts.

**3.** Bake 35 to 40 minutes or until toothpick inserted into center of cake comes out clean. Cool at least 15 minutes before serving.

*Makes 12 to 16 servings*

# CRANBERRY PEAR SPICE CAKE

    1  can (29 ounces) pear slices in light syrup, undrained
    1  package (12 ounces) fresh or thawed frozen cranberries
    1  package (about 15 ounces) spice cake mix
    ½  cup (1 stick) butter, cut into thin slices
    1  cup chopped walnuts
       Whipped cream (optional)

1. Preheat oven to 350°F. Spray 13×9-inch baking pan with nonstick cooking spray.

2. Drain ½ cup syrup from pears. Pour remaining pears and syrup into prepared pan; cut pears into 1-inch pieces with paring knife or scissors. Spread cranberries over pears. Top with cake mix, spreading evenly. Top with butter in single layer, covering cake mix as much as possible. Sprinkle with walnuts.

3. Bake 40 to 45 minutes or until toothpick inserted into center of cake comes out clean. Cool at least 15 minutes before serving. Serve with whipped cream, if desired.

*Makes 12 to 16 servings*

# CARROT BANANA CAKE

- 1 package (about 15 ounces) carrot cake mix, plus ingredients to prepare mix
- 1 teaspoon baking soda
- 2 bananas, mashed (about 1 heaping cup)
- 1 cup chopped walnuts
- ½ cup raisins

    Prepared cream cheese frosting, warmed (optional)

    Additional chopped walnuts (optional)

1. Preheat oven to 350°F. Grease and flour 12-cup (10-inch) bundt pan.

2. Prepare cake mix according to package directions. Stir baking soda into mashed bananas; add to batter and beat until well blended. Stir in 1 cup walnuts and raisins. Pour into prepared pan.

3. Bake 40 to 45 minutes or until toothpick inserted near center comes out clean. Cool in pan 10 minutes; invert onto wire rack to cool completely.

4. Drizzle cream cheese frosting over cooled cake and sprinkle with additional walnuts, if desired.

*Makes 12 servings*

# AUTUMN DUMP CAKE

1 can (29 ounces) pear slices in light syrup, undrained

1 can (21 ounces) apple pie filling

½ cup dried cranberries

1 package (about 15 ounces) yellow cake mix

½ cup (1 stick) butter, cut into thin slices

¼ cup caramel topping, warmed

1. Preheat oven to 350°F. Spray 13×9-inch baking pan with nonstick cooking spray.

2. Drain pears, reserving ½ cup syrup. Spread pears and apple pie filling in prepared pan; drizzle with reserved syrup. Sprinkle with cranberries. Top with cake mix, spreading evenly. Top with butter in single layer, covering cake mix as much as possible. Drizzle with caramel topping.

3. Bake 40 to 45 minutes or until toothpick inserted into center of cake comes out clean. Cool at least 15 minutes before serving.

*Makes 12 to 16 servings*

# Pumpkin Chocolate Chip Cake

- 1 package (about 15 ounces) spice cake mix
- 1 can (15 ounces) solid-pack pumpkin
- 2 eggs
- ⅓ cup water
- 1 cup semisweet chocolate chips
- 1 cup semisweet chocolate chips, melted (optional)

**1.** Preheat oven to 350°F. Grease and flour 12-cup (10-inch) bundt pan.

**2.** Combine cake mix, pumpkin, eggs and water in large bowl; beat 1 to 2 minutes or until well blended. Stir in 1 cup chocolate chips. Pour batter into prepared pan.

**3.** Bake 35 to 40 minutes or until toothpick inserted near center comes out clean. Cool in pan 10 minutes; invert onto wire rack to cool completely.

**4.** Drizzle melted chocolate over cooled cake, if desired.

*Makes 12 servings*

# EASY
## ANYTIME CAKES

## CRUNCHY PEACH SNACK CAKE

- 1 package (9 ounces) yellow cake mix
- 1 container (6 ounces) peach yogurt
- 1 egg
- ¼ cup peach fruit spread
- ¾ cup square cinnamon multigrain cereal, slightly crushed

  Whipped cream (optional)

1. Preheat oven to 350°F. Spray 8-inch square baking pan with nonstick cooking spray.

2. Combine cake mix, yogurt and egg in large bowl; beat with electric mixer at low speed until blended. Beat at medium speed 2 minutes or until smooth.

3. Spread batter in prepared pan. Drop fruit spread by ½ teaspoonfuls over top. Sprinkle with cereal.

4. Bake 25 minutes or until toothpick inserted into center comes out clean. Cool completely in pan on wire rack. Serve with whipped cream, if desired.

*Makes 9 servings*

# Simple Strawberry Cake

1 package (about 15 ounces) white cake mix

1 package (4-serving size) strawberry gelatin

2 containers (6 ounces each) strawberry yogurt

4 eggs

⅓ cup vegetable or canola oil

1 container (8 ounces) thawed frozen whipped topping, divided

Fresh strawberries (optional)

**1.** Preheat oven to 350°F. Spray 13×9-inch baking pan with nonstick cooking spray.

**2.** Combine cake mix, gelatin, yogurt, eggs and oil in large bowl; beat with electric mixer at low speed about 1 minute or until blended. Beat at medium speed 2 minutes or until smooth. Spread batter in prepared pan.

**3.** Bake 35 to 40 minutes or until toothpick inserted into center comes out clean. Cool completely in pan on wire rack.

**4.** Spread whipped topping over cooled cake. Decorate with strawberries, if desired. Serve immediately or cover loosely and refrigerate up to 24 hours.

*Makes 12 to 16 servings*

# ORANGE POUND CAKE

   1  **medium orange**

   1  **package (16 ounces) pound cake mix**

   2  **eggs**

**1.** Preheat oven to 350°F. Grease and flour 8×4-inch loaf pan.

**2.** Finely grate orange peel. Juice orange; add enough water to equal ¾ cup.

**3.** Combine cake mix, eggs, orange peel and orange juice mixture in large bowl; beat with electric mixer at medium speed 2 minutes or until well blended. Pour batter into prepared pan.

**4.** Bake 50 to 55 minutes or until toothpick inserted into center comes out clean. Cool in pan 10 minutes; remove to wire rack to cool completely.

*Makes 12 servings*

TIP: Wrap leftover pound cake slices tightly in plastic wrap, place in a resealable food storage bag and freeze.

# CHOCOLATE MYSTERY CAKE

    1  **package (about 15 ounces) German chocolate cake mix**

  1½  **cups plus 2 tablespoons root beer (not diet), divided**

    2  **eggs**

  ¼  **cup vegetable or canola oil**

    1  **container (about 16 ounces) vanilla frosting**

**1.** Preheat oven to 350°F. Spray 13×9-inch baking pan with nonstick cooking spray.

**2.** Combine cake mix, 1½ cups root beer, eggs and oil in large bowl; beat with electric mixer at low speed 30 seconds. Beat at medium speed 2 minutes or until well blended. Spread batter in prepared pan.

**3.** Bake 30 minutes or until toothpick inserted into center comes out clean. Cool completely in pan on wire rack.

**4.** Beat remaining 2 tablespoons root beer into frosting until well blended. Spread frosting over cooled cake.

*Makes 12 to 16 servings*

# Pineapple Coffeecake

1¾ cups biscuit baking mix

1 container (6 ounces) vanilla yogurt

1 egg

¼ cup granulated sugar

2 tablespoons vegetable or canola oil

1 teaspoon grated fresh ginger

1 teaspoon vanilla

2 cans (8 ounces each) pineapple tidbits, drained

⅓ cup packed dark brown sugar

1. Preheat oven to 375°F. Spray 9-inch round nonstick cake pan or springform pan with nonstick cooking spray.

2. Combine baking mix, yogurt, egg, granulated sugar, oil, ginger and vanilla in large bowl; mix well. (Batter will be lumpy.) Spread batter in prepared pan; top with pineapple and brown sugar.

3. Bake 25 minutes or until toothpick inserted into center comes out almost clean. If desired, place cake under broiler about 1 minute or until top is browned. Let stand 10 to 15 minutes. Invert cake onto plate, then invert again onto serving plate. Serve warm or at room temperature.

*Makes 9 servings*

# GINGER SWEET POTATO CAKE

   1  **package (about 18 ounces) spice cake mix**
   1  **can (15 ounces) sweet potatoes, drained and mashed**
1⅓  **cups water**
   3  **eggs**
   2  **tablespoons vegetable or canola oil**
   1  **tablespoon grated fresh ginger**
   1  **container (8 ounces) thawed frozen whipped topping**

**1.** Preheat oven to 350°F. Spray 13×9-inch baking pan with nonstick cooking spray.

**2.** Combine cake mix, sweet potatoes, water, eggs, oil and ginger in large bowl; beat 2 minutes or until well blended. Spread batter in prepared pan.

**3.** Bake 30 minutes or until toothpick inserted into center comes out clean. Cool completely in pan on wire rack.

**4.** Spread whipped topping over cooled cake. Cover and refrigerate until ready to serve.

*Makes 12 to 16 servings*

# CITRUSY POUND CAKES

       2  packages (16 ounces each) pound cake mix

       4  eggs

       1  cup water

       ½  cup orange juice

       2  tablespoons lemon juice

       2  teaspoons grated lemon peel

       2  teaspoons grated orange peel

          Citrus Glaze (recipe follows, optional)

1. Preheat oven to 350°F. Spray six mini (5×3-inch) loaf pans with nonstick cooking spray. Place on baking sheet.

2. Combine cake mixes, eggs, water, orange juice, lemon juice, lemon peel and orange peel in large bowl; beat 2 minutes or until well blended. Pour 1 cup batter into each prepared pan.

3. Bake 45 minutes or until toothpick inserted into centers comes out clean. Cool completely in pans on wire racks.

4. Prepare Citrus Glaze, if desired. Drizzle glaze over cooled cakes; let stand until set.

*Makes 6 mini cakes*

CITRUS GLAZE: Combine 1 cup powdered sugar, 1 tablespoon orange juice and ½ teaspoon vanilla, if desired, in small bowl; whisk until smooth. Add additional juice, if necessary, to reach desired consistency.

# German Upside Down Cake

    1½  cups flaked coconut

     1  cup chopped pecans

     1  container (16 ounces) coconut pecan frosting

     1  package (about 15 ounces) German chocolate
        cake mix

    1⅓  cups water

     4  eggs

     ⅓  cup vegetable or canola oil

     1  cup milk chocolate chips

1. Preheat oven to 350°F. Spray 13×9-inch glass baking dish with nonstick cooking spray.

2. Spread coconut evenly in prepared dish. Sprinkle pecans over coconut. Drop frosting by tablespoonfuls over pecans. (Do not spread.)

3. Combine cake mix, water, eggs and oil in large bowl; beat with electric mixer at low speed 30 seconds. Beat at medium speed 2 minutes or until well blended. Stir in chocolate chips. Spread batter in dish over frosting.

4. Bake 35 minutes or until toothpick inserted into center comes out clean. Cool in dish 10 minutes; invert onto serving plate. Serve warm.

*Makes 12 to 16 servings*

# FAVORITE POTLUCK CARROT CAKE

- 1 package (about 15 ounces) yellow cake mix
- 1 package (4-serving size) vanilla instant pudding and pie filling mix
- 3 cups grated carrots
- 1 can (8 ounces) crushed pineapple, undrained
- 4 eggs
- ½ cup chopped walnuts
- ½ cup water
- 2 teaspoons ground cinnamon
- 1 container (16 ounces) cream cheese frosting

1. Preheat oven to 350°F. Spray 13×9-inch baking pan with nonstick cooking spray.

2. Combine cake mix, pudding mix, carrots, pineapple, eggs, walnuts, water and cinnamon in large bowl; beat with electric mixer at low speed 30 seconds. Beat at medium speed 2 minutes or until well blended. Spread batter in prepared pan.

3. Bake 40 to 45 minutes or until toothpick inserted into center comes out clean. Cool completely in pan on wire rack.

4. Spread frosting over cooled cake.

*Makes 12 to 16 servings*

# Rocky Road Cake

    1  package (about 15 ounces) devil's food cake mix

1⅓  cups water

    3  eggs

    ½  cup vegetable or canola oil

    2  teaspoons instant coffee granules (optional)

    4  cups mini marshmallows

    1  cup chopped walnuts or pecans, toasted*

    1  container (16 ounces) hot fudge topping, warmed

*To toast walnuts, spread in single layer on baking sheet. Bake in preheated 350°F oven 5 to 7 minutes or until lightly browned, stirring frequently.*

1. Preheat oven to 350°F. Spray 13×9-inch baking pan with nonstick cooking spray.

2. Combine cake mix, water, eggs, oil and coffee granules, if desired, in large bowl; beat with electric mixer at medium speed 2 minutes or until well blended. Spread batter in prepared pan.

3. Bake 30 minutes or until toothpick inserted into center comes out almost clean. Immediately sprinkle marshmallows over cake; top with walnuts. Cool in pan 15 minutes.

4. Drizzle hot fudge topping over cake; cool completely.

*Makes 12 to 16 servings*

# Pineapple Coconut Pound Cake

- 1 package (about 15 ounces) yellow cake mix
- 1 package (4-serving size) cheesecake instant pudding and pie filling mix
- 1 can (8 ounces) crushed pineapple, undrained
- 3 eggs
- ½ cup water
- ¼ cup vegetable or canola oil
- 1 cup flaked coconut
  Whipped cream (optional)

**1.** Preheat oven to 350°F. Spray two 8×4-inch loaf pans with nonstick cooking spray.

**2.** Combine cake mix, pudding mix, pineapple, eggs, water and oil in large bowl; beat with electric mixer at medium speed 2 minutes or until well blended. Stir in coconut. Pour batter into prepared pans.

**3.** Bake 45 to 50 minutes or until toothpick inserted into centers comes out clean. Cool in pans 10 minutes; remove to wire racks to cool completely. Serve with whipped cream, if desired.

*Makes 24 servings*

# TRIPLE CHOCOLATE PUDDING CAKE

  1  **cup biscuit baking mix**

  ½  **cup sugar**

  ¼  **cup unsweetened cocoa powder**

  ¾  **cup milk, divided**

  ⅓  **cup butter, softened**

  ¾  **cup hot fudge topping, divided**

  1  **teaspoon vanilla**

  1  **cup semisweet chocolate chips, divided**

  ¾  **cup coffee or hot water**

   **Fresh raspberries or whipped cream (optional)**

**1.** Preheat oven to 350°F. Spray 8-inch square baking pan with nonstick cooking spray.

**2.** Combine baking mix, sugar and cocoa in medium bowl; mix well. Add ½ cup milk, butter, ¼ cup hot fudge topping and vanilla; beat until well blended. Stir in ½ cup chocolate chips. Pour batter into prepared pan.

**3.** Combine remaining ¼ cup milk, ½ cup hot fudge topping and coffee in same bowl; stir until well blended. Pour over batter in pan. *Do not stir.* Sprinkle with remaining ½ cup chocolate chips.

**4.** Bake 45 to 50 minutes or until set. Cool in pan on wire rack 15 minutes. Serve warm; garnish with raspberries.

*Makes 8 servings*

# Butter Brickle Cake

- 2 teaspoons ground cinnamon
- ⅔ cup sugar
- 1 package (about 15 ounces) yellow cake mix
- 1 package (4-serving size) butterscotch instant pudding and pie filling mix
- 4 eggs
- ¾ cup vegetable oil
- ¾ cup water
- 1 cup chopped walnuts, divided

**1.** Preheat oven to 350°F. Grease and flour 13×9-inch baking pan. Stir cinnamon into sugar until blended.

**2.** Beat cake mix, pudding mix, eggs, oil and water in large bowl with electric mixer at medium speed 5 minutes or until fluffy. Pour half of batter into prepared pan. Sprinkle with ½ cup walnuts and half of cinnamon-sugar. Top with remaining batter; sprinkle with remaining walnuts and cinnamon-sugar.

**3.** Bake 40 minutes or until toothpick inserted into center comes out clean. Cool in pan on wire rack. Serve warm or at room temperature.

*Makes 12 to 16 servings*

SERVING SUGGESTION: Serve with whipped cream or vanilla ice cream.

# CRANBERRY CHOCOLATE CAKE

  1  **package (about 15 ounces) devil's food cake mix**

1⅓  **cups water**

  3  **eggs**

  ½  **cup vegetable oil**

  1  **can (16 ounces) whole berry cranberry sauce, divided**

  2  **tablespoons unsweetened cocoa powder**

  1  **container (8 ounces) thawed frozen whipped topping**

  1  **cup sliced almonds, toasted***

*\*To toast almonds, spread in single layer on baking sheet. Bake in preheated 350°F oven 5 to 7 minutes or until lightly browned, stirring occasionally.*

**1.** Preheat oven to 350°F. Grease bottom only of 13×9-inch baking pan.

**2.** Combine cake mix, water, eggs and oil in large bowl; beat with electric mixer at low speed 30 seconds. Beat at medium speed 2 minutes or until blended. Add half of cranberry sauce; beat until well blended. Pour batter into prepared pan.

**3.** Bake about 30 minutes or until toothpick inserted into center comes out clean. Cool completely in pan on wire rack.

**4.** Sift cocoa over whipped topping; fold until mixture is well blended.

**5.** Microwave remaining cranberry sauce on HIGH 15 seconds or until softened. Spread evenly over cake; top with whipped topping mixture. Cover and refrigerate until ready to serve. Sprinkle with almonds just before serving.

*Makes 12 to 16 servings*

# Banana Poppy Seed Cake

1 package (about 15 ounces) white cake mix

1 package (4-serving size) banana cream-flavor instant pudding and pie filling mix

1 cup water

⅔ cup applesauce

4 egg whites

¼ cup poppy seeds

**1.** Preheat oven to 350°F. Spray 17×12-inch jelly-roll pan with nonstick cooking spray.

**2.** Combine cake mix, pudding mix, water, applesauce, egg whites and poppy seeds in large bowl; beat 2 minutes or until well blended. Pour batter into prepared pan.

**3.** Bake 18 minutes or until toothpick inserted into center comes out clean. Serve warm or cool completely in pan on wire rack.

*Makes 20 to 24 servings*

# TORTOISE SNACK CAKE

  1  package (about 15 ounces) devil's food cake mix

1¼  cups water

  3  eggs

½  cup vegetable or canola oil

  1  cup chopped pecans

  1  cup semisweet chocolate chips

½  teaspoon vanilla

½  cup caramel sauce

   Additional caramel sauce and chopped pecans
   (optional)

**1.** Preheat oven to 350°F. Spray 13×9-inch baking pan with nonstick cooking spray.

**2.** Combine cake mix, water, eggs and oil in large bowl; beat with electric mixer at low speed 30 seconds. Beat at medium speed 2 minutes or until well blended. Stir in 1 cup pecans, chocolate chips and vanilla. Pour batter into prepared pan. Drizzle ½ cup caramel sauce over batter; swirl into batter with knife.

**3.** Bake about 30 minutes or until toothpick inserted into center comes out clean. Cool in pan on wire rack 15 minutes.

**4.** Top each serving with additional caramel sauce and pecans, if desired.

*Makes 12 to 16 servings*

# ONE-BOWL
## BUNDT CAKES

### BUTTERSCOTCH BUNDT CAKE

- 1 package (about 15 ounces) yellow cake mix
- 1 package (4-serving size) butterscotch instant pudding and pie filling mix
- 1 cup water
- 3 eggs
- 2 teaspoons ground cinnamon
- ½ cup chopped pecans
- Powdered sugar (optional)

1. Preheat oven to 325°F. Spray 12-cup (10-inch) bundt pan with nonstick cooking spray.

2. Combine cake mix, pudding mix, water, eggs and cinnamon in large bowl; beat with electric mixer at medium speed 2 minutes or until well blended. Stir in pecans. Pour batter into prepared pan.

3. Bake 40 to 50 minutes or until cake springs back when lightly touched. Cool in pan 10 minutes; invert onto serving plate to cool completely.

4. Sprinkle with powdered sugar just before serving, if desired.

*Makes 12 servings*

# Coconut Almond Cake

1 package (about 15 ounces) yellow cake mix

1 package (4-serving size) vanilla instant pudding
   and pie filling mix

4 eggs

1 cup sour cream

¾ cup water

¼ cup vegetable or canola oil

½ teaspoon coconut extract

½ teaspoon vanilla

½ cup sliced almonds, toasted and chopped

⅓ cup flaked coconut

Chocolate Ganache (recipe follows, optional)

Additional sliced almonds and coconut (optional)

1. Preheat oven to 350°F. Spray 10- or 12-cup bundt pan with nonstick cooking spray.

2. Combine cake mix, pudding mix, eggs, sour cream, water, oil, coconut extract and vanilla in large bowl; beat with electric mixer at low speed 30 seconds. Beat at medium speed 2 minutes or until smooth. Stir in chopped almonds and coconut. Pour batter into prepared pan.

3. Bake 1 hour or until toothpick inserted near center comes out clean. Cool in pan 10 minutes; invert onto wire rack to cool completely.

4. Prepare Chocolate Ganache, if desired. Spoon ganache over cooled cake; sprinkle with additional almonds and coconut.

*Makes 12 servings*

CHOCOLATE GANACHE: Heat ½ cup whipping cream in small saucepan just until hot (do not boil). Remove from heat; add ½ cup semisweet chocolate chips and let stand 2 minutes. Whisk until smooth. Let stand at room temperature 15 to 20 minutes or until slightly thickened.

# APPLE BUTTER CAKE

- 1 package (about 15 ounces) yellow cake mix
- 1 package (4-serving size) vanilla instant pudding and pie filling mix
- 1 cup sour cream
- 1 cup apple butter
- 4 eggs
- ½ cup apple juice
- ¼ cup vegetable or canola oil
- 1 teaspoon ground cinnamon
- ½ teaspoon ground nutmeg
- ½ teaspoon ground cloves
- ¼ teaspoon salt
- Powdered sugar (optional)

**1.** Preheat oven to 375°F. Spray 10-inch tube or bundt pan with nonstick cooking spray.

**2.** Combine cake mix, pudding mix, sour cream, apple butter, eggs, apple juice, oil, cinnamon, nutmeg, cloves and salt in large bowl; beat with electric mixer at low speed 1 minute. Beat at medium speed 2 minutes or until well blended. Pour batter into prepared pan.

**3.** Bake 45 to 50 minutes or until toothpick inserted near center comes out clean. Cool in pan 20 minutes. Run sharp knife along edge of pan to release cake; invert cake onto serving plate. Cool completely.

**4.** Just before serving, if desired, place 9-inch paper doily over cake. Sift powdered sugar over doily; carefully remove doily.

*Makes 12 servings*

# ZUCCHINI SPICE CAKE

- 1 package (about 15 ounces) spice or carrot cake mix
- 1 cup water
- 3 eggs
- 2 tablespoons vegetable or canola oil
- 1 medium zucchini, shredded
- ¼ cup chopped walnuts, toasted*
- ¾ teaspoon vanilla
- Glaze (recipe follows, optional)

*To toast walnuts, spread in single layer on baking sheet. Bake in preheated 350°F oven 5 to 7 minutes or until golden brown, stirring frequently.*

**1.** Preheat oven to 325°F. Spray 12-cup (10-inch) bundt pan with nonstick cooking spray.

**2.** Combine cake mix, water, eggs and oil in large bowl; beat 2 minutes or until well blended. Stir in zucchini, walnuts and vanilla until blended. Pour batter into prepared pan.

**3.** Bake 40 minutes or until toothpick inserted near center comes out almost clean. Cool in pan 10 minutes; invert onto wire rack to cool completely.

**4.** Prepare Glaze, if desired. Drizzle glaze over cooled cake; let stand until set.

*Makes 12 to 16 servings*

GLAZE: Combine ¼ cup powdered sugar and 1 to 2 teaspoons milk in small bowl; whisk until smooth.

# Chocolate Orange Bundt Cake

   1  package (about 15 ounces) devil's food cake mix

1⅓  cups water

   3  eggs

   ¼  cup vegetable or canola oil

   1  tablespoon instant coffee granules

   1  tablespoon grated orange peel

   1  teaspoon ground cinnamon

      Orange Glaze (recipe follows, optional)

1. Preheat oven to 325°F. Spray 12-cup (10-inch) bundt pan with nonstick cooking spray.

2. Combine cake mix, water, eggs, oil, coffee granules, orange peel and cinnamon in large bowl; beat with electric mixer at medium speed 2 minutes or until well blended. Pour batter into prepared pan.

3. Bake 35 to 40 minutes or until toothpick inserted near center comes out clean. Cool in pan 10 minutes; invert onto wire rack to cool completely.

4. Prepare Orange Glaze, if desired. Drizzle glaze over cooled cake.

*Makes 12 servings*

ORANGE GLAZE: Combine ½ cup orange juice and 1 teaspoon cornstarch in small saucepan; stir until cornstarch is dissolved. Bring to a boil over medium-high heat; boil 1 minute or until thickened. Cool completely.

# Peanut Butter Cookie Cake

1 package (about 15 ounces) white cake mix

1 package (4-serving size) vanilla instant pudding
   and pie filling mix

4 eggs

½ cup milk

⅓ cup vegetable or canola oil

¼ cup water

¼ cup creamy peanut butter

2 cups chopped peanut butter cookies, divided

½ cup semisweet chocolate chips, melted

1. Preheat oven to 350°F. Spray 12-cup (10-inch) bundt pan with nonstick cooking spray.

2. Combine cake mix, pudding mix, eggs, milk, oil, water and peanut butter in large bowl; beat with electric mixer at medium speed 2 minutes or until well blended. Stir in 1¾ cups chopped cookies. Pour batter into prepared pan.

3. Bake 50 to 60 minutes or until cake springs back when lightly touched. Cool in pan 10 minutes; invert onto wire rack to cool completely.

4. Drizzle melted chocolate over cooled cake; sprinkle with remaining ¼ cup chopped cookies.

*Makes 12 servings*

# Lemon Berry Bundt

- 1 package (about 18 ounces) lemon cake mix
- 5 eggs
- 1 cup plain yogurt
- ⅓ cup vegetable or canola oil
- 1 tablespoon grated lemon peel
- 8 ounces frozen unsweetened mixed berries, thawed and patted dry*

    Lemon Glaze (recipe follows, optional)

*Or substitute 1½ cups fresh berries in season; slice strawberries, if used.*

**1.** Preheat oven to 325°F. Spray 12-cup (10-inch) bundt pan with nonstick cooking spray.

**2.** Combine cake mix, eggs, yogurt, oil and lemon peel in large bowl; beat with electric mixer at low speed 30 seconds. Beat at medium speed 2 minutes. Pour half of batter into prepared pan; sprinkle with berries. Pour remaining batter over berries.

**3.** Bake 50 to 55 minutes or until toothpick inserted near center comes out clean. Cool in pan 15 minutes. Gently loosen edge and center of cake with knife; invert onto wire rack.

**4.** Prepare Lemon Glaze, if desired. Spoon glaze over warm cake. Serve warm or at room temperature.

*Makes 12 servings*

LEMON GLAZE: Combine 1 cup powdered sugar, 2 tablespoons melted butter, 2 tablespoons lemon juice and 1 teaspoon vanilla in small bowl; whisk until smooth.

# Mandarin Orange Tea Cake

    1  package (16 ounces) pound cake mix

    ½  cup orange juice

    2  eggs

    ¼  cup milk

    1  can (15 ounces) mandarin orange segments
       in light syrup, drained

       Orange Glaze (recipe follows, optional)

**1.** Preheat oven to 350°F. Spray 9-inch bundt pan with nonstick cooking spray.

**2.** Combine cake mix, orange juice, eggs and milk in large bowl; beat with electric mixer at medium speed 2 minutes or until well blended. Stir in orange segments. Pour batter into prepared pan.

**3.** Bake 45 minutes or until golden brown and toothpick inserted near center comes out clean. Cool in pan 15 minutes; invert onto wire rack to cool completely.

**4.** Prepare Orange Glaze, if desired. Drizzle glaze over cooled cake; let stand until set.

*Makes 12 servings*

ORANGE GLAZE: Combine ¾ cup powdered sugar, 2 tablespoons orange juice and grated peel of 1 orange in small bowl; whisk until smooth.

# APPLE SPICE CAKE

1 can (21 ounces) apple pie filling

1 package (about 15 ounces) spice cake mix

2 teaspoons ground cinnamon

3 eggs

Glaze (recipe follows, optional)

**1.** Preheat oven to 350°F. Grease and flour 12-cup (10-inch) bundt pan.

**2.** Place apple pie filling in large bowl; cut apples into ¼-inch pieces with paring knife or scissors. Add cake mix, cinnamon and eggs; beat with electric mixer at low speed 30 seconds. Beat at medium speed 2 minutes or until well blended. Pour batter into prepared pan.

**3.** Bake 45 to 55 minutes or until toothpick inserted near center of cake comes out clean. Cool in pan on wire rack 1 hour. Invert onto serving plate.

**3.** Prepare Glaze, if desired. Drizzle glaze over cooled cake.

*Makes 12 servings*

GLAZE: Combine 1 cup powdered sugar, 2 teaspoons milk and ½ teaspoon vanilla in small bowl; whisk until smooth.

# Cookies 'n' Cream Cake

    1  package (about 15 ounces) white cake mix
    1  package (4-serving size) white chocolate instant
       pudding and pie filling mix
    1  cup vegetable or canola oil
    4  egg whites
    ½  cup milk
   20  chocolate sandwich cookies, coarsely chopped
    ½  cup semisweet chocolate chips, melted
    4  chocolate sandwich cookies, cut into quarters

1. Preheat oven to 350°F. Spray 12-cup (10-inch) bundt pan
with nonstick cooking spray.

2. Combine cake mix, pudding mix, oil, egg whites and
milk in large bowl; beat with electric mixer at medium
speed 2 minutes or until well blended. Stir in chopped
cookies. Pour batter into prepared pan.

3. Bake 50 to 60 minutes or until cake springs back
when lightly touched. Cool in pan on wire rack 1 hour;
invert onto serving plate to cool completely.

4. Drizzle melted chocolate over cooled cake; top with
quartered cookies.

*Makes 12 servings*

# PECAN PRALINE BRANDY CAKE

- 1 package (about 15 ounces) butter pecan cake mix
- ¾ cup water
- ⅓ cup plain yogurt
- 2 egg whites
- 1 egg
- ¼ cup brandy
- 2 tablespoons vegetable oil
- ½ cup chopped toasted pecans*

  Praline Glaze (recipe follows, optional)

*To toast pecans, spread in single layer on baking sheet. Bake in 350°F oven 6 to 8 minutes or until lightly browned, stirring frequently.*

**1.** Preheat oven to 350°F. Spray 10- or 12-cup bundt pan with nonstick cooking spray.

**2.** Beat cake mix, water, yogurt, egg whites, egg, brandy and oil in medium bowl with electric mixer at low speed 30 seconds. Beat at medium speed 2 minutes or until light and fluffy. Fold in pecans. Pour batter into prepared pan.

**3.** Bake 50 minutes or until toothpick inserted near center comes out clean. Cool in pan 10 minutes; invert onto wire rack to cool completely.

**4.** Prepare Praline Glaze, if desired. Place cake on serving plate. Pour glaze over cake; let stand until set.

*Makes 12 servings*

Praline Glaze: Combine ⅔ cup packed brown sugar, ⅓ cup light corn syrup, ¼ cup whipping cream and 2 tablespoons butter in small saucepan; bring to a boil over medium heat, stirring constantly. Remove from heat; stir in ½ cup chopped toasted pecans, ½ teaspoon brandy and ½ teaspoon vanilla. Cool to room temperature.

# Mango-Orange Pound Cake

1 package (about 16 ounces) pound cake mix,
  plus ingredients to prepare mix

2 ripe mangoes, peeled and diced (about 2 cups),
  divided

1 teaspoon grated orange peel

Orange Vanilla Glaze (recipe follows, optional)

**1.** Preheat oven to 350°F. Grease and flour 9-cup nonstick bundt pan.

**2.** Prepare cake mix according to package directions; stir in ½ cup mango and orange peel. Pour batter into prepared pan.

**3.** Bake 36 to 40 minutes or until toothpick inserted near center comes out clean. Cool in pan 10 minutes; invert onto wire rack to cool completely.

**4.** Prepare Orange Vanilla Glaze, if desired. Place cake on serving plate. Drizzle glaze over cake; sprinkle with remaining 1½ cups mango.

*Makes 10 servings*

ORANGE VANILLA GLAZE: Combine 1½ cups powdered sugar, 2 to 3 teaspoons orange juice, ½ teaspoon vanilla and ¼ teaspoon coconut extract, if desired, in small bowl; whisk until smooth.

# DOUBLE CHOCOLATE BUNDT CAKE

- 1 package (about 15 ounces) chocolate cake mix
- 1 package (4-serving size) chocolate instant pudding and pie filling mix
- 4 eggs
- ¾ cup water
- ¾ cup sour cream
- ½ cup vegetable or canola oil
- 1 cup semisweet chocolate chips
- Powdered sugar

**1.** Preheat oven to 350°F. Spray 12-cup (10-inch) bundt or tube pan with nonstick cooking spray.

**2.** Combine cake mix, pudding mix, eggs, water, sour cream and oil in large bowl; beat with electric mixer at medium speed 2 minutes or until well blended. Stir in chocolate chips. Pour batter into prepared pan.

**3.** Bake 55 to 60 minutes or until cake springs back when lightly touched. Cool in pan on wire rack 1 hour; invert onto serving plate to cool completely.

**4.** Sprinkle with powdered sugar just before serving.

*Makes 12 servings*

# METRIC
## CONVERSION CHART

### VOLUME MEASUREMENTS (dry)

1/8 teaspoon = 0.5 mL
1/4 teaspoon = 1 mL
1/2 teaspoon = 2 mL
3/4 teaspoon = 4 mL
1 teaspoon = 5 mL
1 tablespoon = 15 mL
2 tablespoons = 30 mL
1/4 cup = 60 mL
1/3 cup = 75 mL
1/2 cup = 125 mL
2/3 cup = 150 mL
3/4 cup = 175 mL
1 cup = 250 mL
2 cups = 1 pint = 500 mL
3 cups = 750 mL
4 cups = 1 quart = 1 L

### VOLUME MEASUREMENTS (fluid)

1 fluid ounce (2 tablespoons) = 30 mL
4 fluid ounces (1/2 cup) = 125 mL
8 fluid ounces (1 cup) = 250 mL
12 fluid ounces (1 1/2 cups) = 375 mL
16 fluid ounces (2 cups) = 500 mL

### WEIGHTS (mass)

1/2 ounce = 15 g
1 ounce = 30 g
3 ounces = 90 g
4 ounces = 120 g
8 ounces = 225 g
10 ounces = 285 g
12 ounces = 360 g
16 ounces = 1 pound = 450 g

### DIMENSIONS

1/16 inch = 2 mm
1/8 inch = 3 mm
1/4 inch = 6 mm
1/2 inch = 1.5 cm
3/4 inch = 2 cm
1 inch = 2.5 cm

### OVEN TEMPERATURES

250°F = 120°C
275°F = 140°C
300°F = 150°C
325°F = 160°C
350°F = 180°C
375°F = 190°C
400°F = 200°C
425°F = 220°C
450°F = 230°C

### BAKING PAN SIZES

| Utensil | Size in Inches/Quarts | Metric Volume | Size in Centimeters |
|---|---|---|---|
| Baking or Cake Pan (square or rectangular) | 8×8×2 | 2 L | 20×20×5 |
| | 9×9×2 | 2.5 L | 23×23×5 |
| | 12×8×2 | 3 L | 30×20×5 |
| | 13×9×2 | 3.5 L | 33×23×5 |
| Loaf Pan | 8×4×3 | 1.5 L | 20×10×7 |
| | 9×5×3 | 2 L | 23×13×7 |
| Round Layer Cake Pan | 8×1½ | 1.2 L | 20×4 |
| | 9×1½ | 1.5 L | 23×4 |
| Pie Plate | 8×1¼ | 750 mL | 20×3 |
| | 9×1¼ | 1 L | 23×3 |
| Baking Dish or Casserole | 1 quart | 1 L | — |
| | 1½ quarts | 1.5 L | — |
| | 2 quarts | 2 L | — |